the BRACELET

Written by Heather Penny, Ph.D.   Illustrated by Meredith Carty

Heather!
I love your name! :)
May feel the clarity,
Confidence & courage you
need to step into the
life you were made for!
Cheering you on,
Heather

ISBN: 978-1-4834-5557-0 (sc)
ISBN: 978-1-4834-5558-7 (e)

Because of the dynamic nature of the Internet, any web addresses or links contained in this book may have changed since publication and may no longer be valid. The views expressed in this work are solely those of the author and do not necessarily reflect the views of the publisher, and the publisher hereby disclaims any responsibility for them.

Heather Penny, Ph.D.
D&H Penny, Inc.
Rocklin, CA 95765

www.heatherpenny.com

Lulu Publishing Services rev. date: 8/30/2016

Ordering Information:

Special discounts are available on quantity purchases by corporations, associations, educators, and others. For details, contact the publisher at the above listed website.

U.S. trade bookstores and wholesalers:

Please contact Heather Penny, Ph.D.
Tel: (916) 741.2777
Email: coaching@heatherpenny.com

for Selah ~

My Sweet, Strong & Sensitive daughter.
YOU are one of the best gifts
I have ever received.
This book was always meant
for you... FOR US.

Please remember, you are the
dazzling author of your own story.

Mom ~

There once was a little girl.
She loved to play outside.

She would watch the birds in their nest,
hunt for eggs, create little clubs with
her friends on the great rock, and design
all kinds of beautiful art.

And at night, she would sneak outside
to lie on her back and watch the stars.

In the summer months, she would run through
the grass barefoot and make up games
to play in the evening with her friends.

But her favorite enjoyment was
swinging from the great tree
on her tire swing.

She would climb the hill to the
tree where her tire swing awaited.

And as it carried her back and forth,
she would throw her head back

and feel the breeze on
her face and let it
blow her hair.

And in these moments she felt most free.

The little girl was
gentle and kind...
  yet passionate and wild.

Then one day she received a special gift
from someone who loved her very much.

The giver solemnly
handed her a
beautifully wrapped
box and as she
opened it,

the giver explained
the great
honor bestowed
upon her.

It was a beautiful gold bracelet
    to be worn by the little girl at all times.

For you see, the
little girl was
growing
up and
could
now
handle the
responsibility
that came with
this beautiful gift.

The giver wanted the little girl
    to feel loved and know her invaluable beauty.

And with this gift, came the understanding to honor
both the giver and her self by wearing it at all times.

The little girl took this responsibility
very seriously and she loved her gold bracelet.

She would watch it shimmer
and shine in the
sun and she would
fall asleep
holding it
as it rested
on her arm.

She felt loved, noticed, valuable, and cherished.

As the little girl grew, there were many givers in her life, and with each passing season she received more and more bracelets from givers who loved her and from those that wanted her love.

Her arms grew heavy from the bracelets,
and soon she had to stop
running barefoot through the grass
or playing on her beloved tire swing.

As winter faded into spring, the little girl grew into a young woman. And with this passing, there was great celebration with many more bracelets given to her.

As she opened the many bracelets, she began to feel her joy fade.

She realized that each giver expected her to wear their gift at all times.

She continued to smile and thank the givers,
but inside she began to grow fearful.

She was fearful of dishonoring the givers,
and she was weary from the responsibility of
wearing so many bracelets on her arms.

Already her arms felt heavy,
and with each added bracelet
she was able to do
less
and
less.

But not wanting to hurt the givers
she continued to smile and slide
the bracelets up past her elbows.

And the givers all nodded with
pleasure as they smiled great smiles.

One day, as she was quiet and alone in her room, a beautiful bird outside her window caught her eye and she longed to run outside.

She wanted to follow the bird and find out where it lived, just as she had done often when she was young.

A forgotten longing stirred deep within her.

As she ran outside to explore,
she stopped short from the
weight of all her bracelets.

With a deep sadness,
she stared after the bird
until it was a small spec
in the distance.

After standing still
in the sun for
a long while,
she finally turned back.

She tried again the next day
when the longing rose and
she thought of her tire swing.

She made it to the top of the
hill, but was unable to swing
because of her bracelets.

After other attempts, she stopped trying.
It was impossible to do what she loved with the many
bracelets; however, she dared not take them off.

For she did not want to dishonor her givers,
and she liked how they had begun to make
her feel valuable, cherished, and loved.

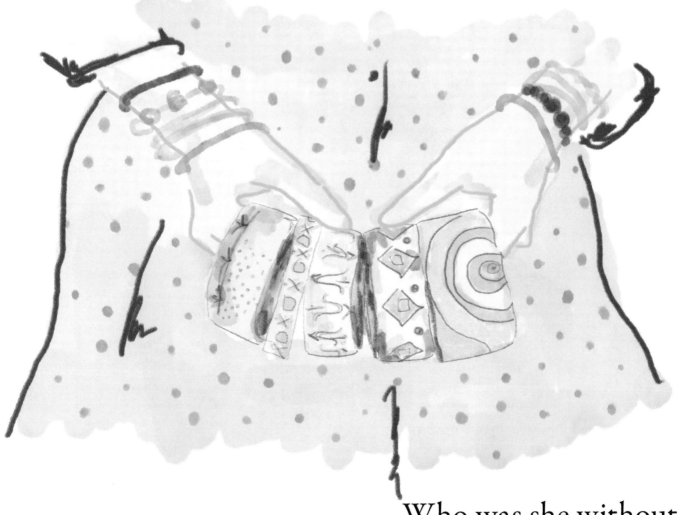

Who was she without
the bracelets?

She no longer knew.

The young woman became dutiful to the expectations
of others and continued to wear the bracelets as
she tried to take comfort in her responsibility.

She stopped looking out the window.
She stopped going outside.
She stopped dreaming of beautiful things.
She stopped playing. She stopped feeling free.

She looked to her givers for love and approval...
and on the inside she began to disappear.

"No one wanted the
little girl who ran free and wild,
no one misses her," she thought.

"I must be a woman with many
bracelets because this is
who people love.
This is now who I am."

So, the young woman became embarrassed of who
she was as a little girl, and collected more and
more bracelets to hide who she had been.

She even began to give them to herself.

But with each passing season,
the sadness within
her grew until she could
contain it no longer.

She longed to stop disappearing
and she longed to be free again.

But most
importantly,
she longed to be
cherished for who
she was before
she had been
given all the
bracelets.

One night, she sneaked outside
and lay under the stars.
As she rested there, she heard a voice on the wind.

"Take off your bracelets...
I did not give them to you."

"Who are you?"
the woman cried.

"I am the Giver of Life,"
responded the voice.

"I give all and I create all.
I created you without
bracelets, and I never
gave you any.

Instead, I gave
you your spirit.

It is a spirit that is
wild, tender, gentle,
and free..."

"Take off your bracelets,
for they dishonor
the greatest gift
you have ever
been given...

your beautiful,
free spirit...

and they
dishonor Me,"
spoke the gentle
voice on
the wind.

It was then that the woman realized
she had a choice to make.

"Shall I take the bracelets off and
risk the displeasure of many?"
she thought.

"Or shall I honor my beautiful spirit and seek the pleasure of the Greatest Giver of All?"

And with that thought, the weary woman fell asleep under the stars asking the Giver of All Good Things to give her the courage to love her greatest gift of all...

her spirit.